I0815516

FIRST WORDS IN...
Hindi
हिन्दी
परिवार
मां
पिता
रात का खाना
by Kirsten Chang
BLASTOFF! READERS
1
BLASTOFF! READERS, AN IMPRINT OF BELLWETHER MEDIA BY FLUTTERBEE

Blastoff! Readers are carefully developed by literacy experts to build reading stamina and move students toward fluency by combining standards-based content with developmentally appropriate text.

Level 1 provides the most support through repetition of high-frequency words, light text, predictable sentence patterns, and strong visual support.

Level 2 offers early readers a bit more challenge through varied sentences, increased text load, and text-supportive special features.

Level 3 advances early-fluent readers toward fluency through increased text load, less reliance on photos, advancing concepts, longer sentences, and more complex special features.

★ **Blastoff! Universe**

Reading Level

Grade K

Grades 1–3

Grade 4

This edition first published in 2026 by Bellwether Media, Inc.

For information regarding permission, write to Bellwether Media, Inc., Attention: Permissions Department, 3500 American Blvd W, Suite 150, Bloomington, MN 55431.

Library of Congress Cataloging-in-Publication Data is available at www.loc.gov or upon request from the publisher.

ISBN: 9798893047769 (hardcover)
ISBN: 9798893048766 (ebook)

Editor: Suzane Nguyen Designer: Andrea Schneider

Printed in the United States of America, North Mankato, MN.

Table of Contents

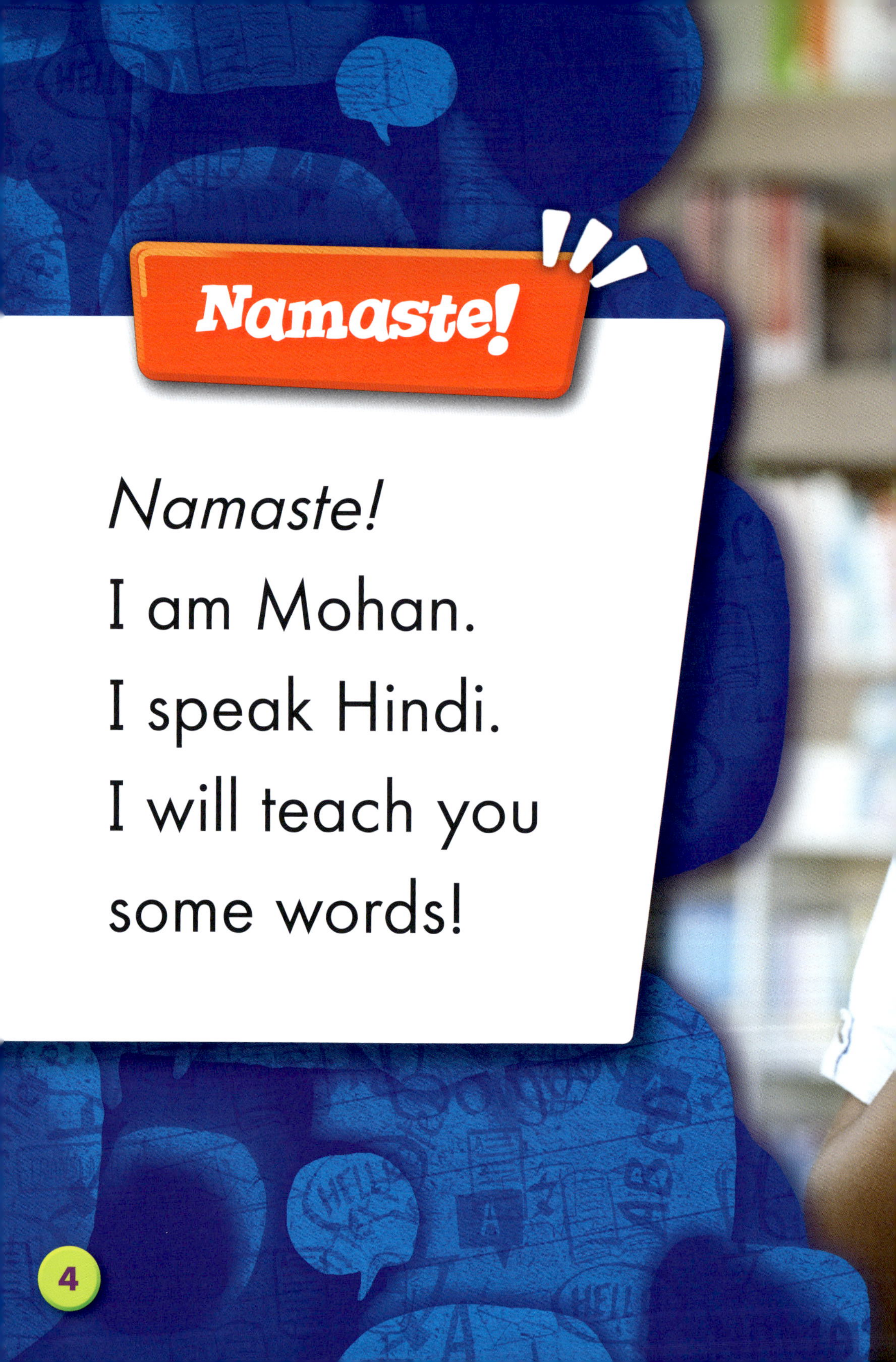

Namaste!

Namaste!
I am Mohan.
I speak Hindi.
I will teach you
some words!

namaste
(nah-mah-STAY)
hello
Words to Know
• हाँ = yes
haan (hahn)
• नही = no
nahin (nah-HEEN)
• कृपया = please
krpaya (krip-YAH)
• हिन्दी = Hindi
hindee (HIN-dee)

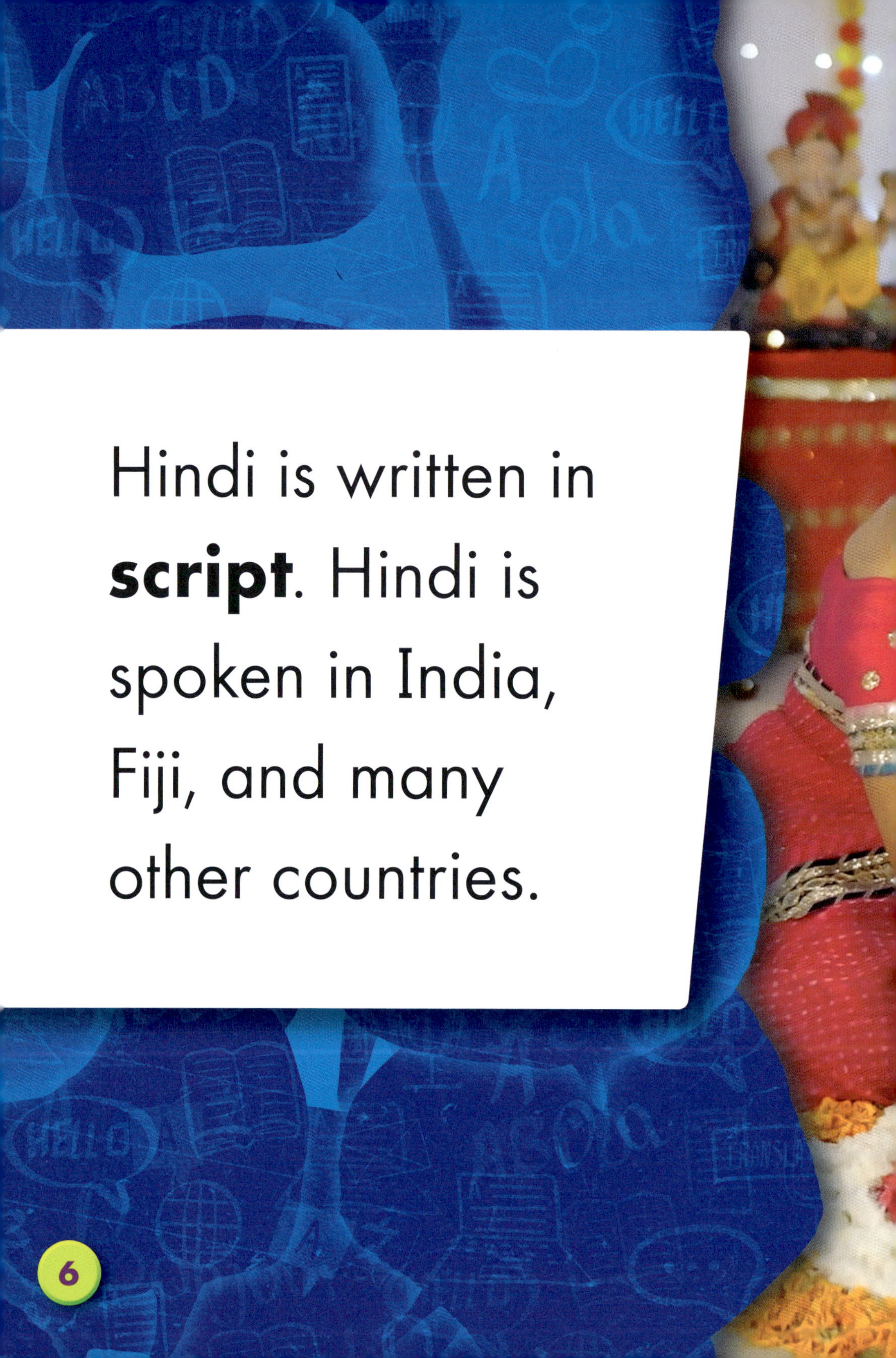

Hindi is written in **script**. Hindi is spoken in India, Fiji, and many other countries.

Hindi-speaking Countries
India
Fiji

At Home

Riya lives with her *parivaar* in their *makaan*. She loves her *kutta*!

Words to Know
• मां = mother
maa (mah)
• पिता = father
pita (pit-AH)
• परिवार = family
parivaar (parr-ee-VAHR)
• मकान = house
makaan (mah-KAHN)
• कुत्ता = dog
kutta (COOT-tah)
pita
maa

Here is Dev's *shayan kaksh*. She likes her *khilauna* bear.

Words to Know

- शयन कक्ष = **bedroom**
  shayan kaksh (shy-AHN kahksh)
- बिस्तर = **bed**
  bistar (biss-TAR)
- खिड़की = **window**
  khidakee (KEER-kee)
- किताब = **book**
  kitaab (kee-TAHB)
- खिलौना = **toy**
  khilauna (kee-LAWN-ah)

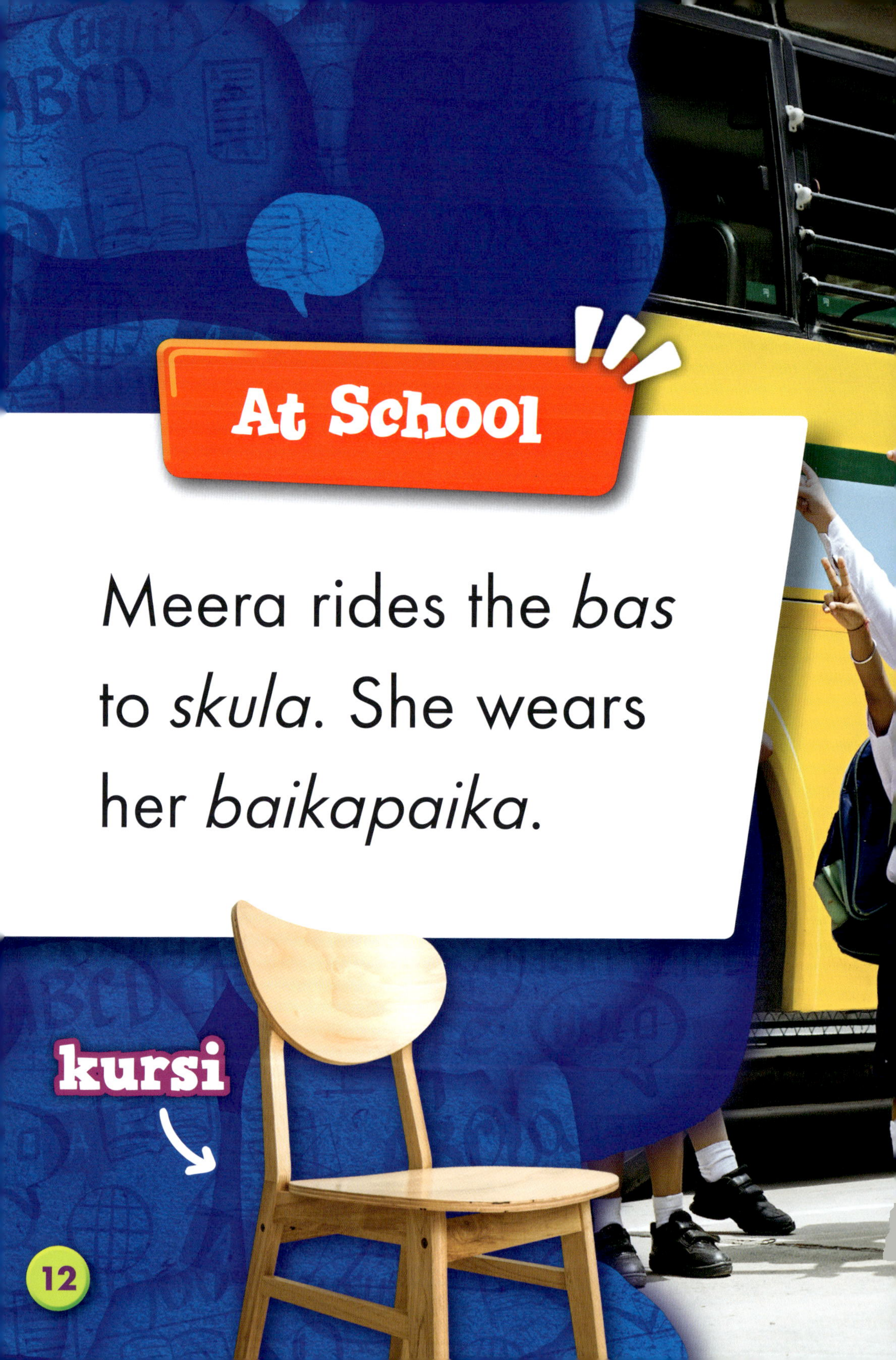

At School

Meera rides the *bas* to *skula*. She wears her *baikapaika*.

Words to Know
• स्कूल = school
skula (SKOOL)
• बैकपैक = backpack
baikapaika (BAK-pak)
• बस = bus
bas (buss)
• कुर्सी = chair
kursi (KOOR-see)
bas
baikapaika

Aryun takes
ganit and *vigyaan*.
He learns **yoga** too.

Count in Hindi

एक.... eek (ayk)............... 1
दो ..... do (doh)......... 2
तीन.... teen (teen)............ 3
चार.... chaar (char)... 4
पांच ... paanch (pahnch)... 5
छह .... che (chay)........ 6
सात ... saat (saht)............. 7
आठ ... aath (ahht).... 8
नौ ..... nau (noh)............... 9
दस..... das (dahs)............ 10

shikshika

Words to Know

- शकिषक = **teacher (male)**
  shikshak (SHICK-shack)
- शकि्षका = **teacher (female)**
  shikshika (SHICK-shick-ah)
- पेंसलि = **pencil**
  pensil (PIN-sill)
- गणति = **math**
  ganit (GAHN-it)
- वज्ञिान = **science**
  vigyaan (vig-YAHN)

For Fun

After school, Vihan plays **cricket** with his *dost*.

Words to Know

- दोस्त = **friend**
  dost (dohst)
- टीम = **team**
  team (teem)
- क्रिकेट की गेंद = **cricket ball**
  kriket kee gend (CREE-ket kee GEEND)
- क्रिकेट का बल्ला = **cricket bat**
  kriket ka balla (CREE-ket kah BAH-lah)

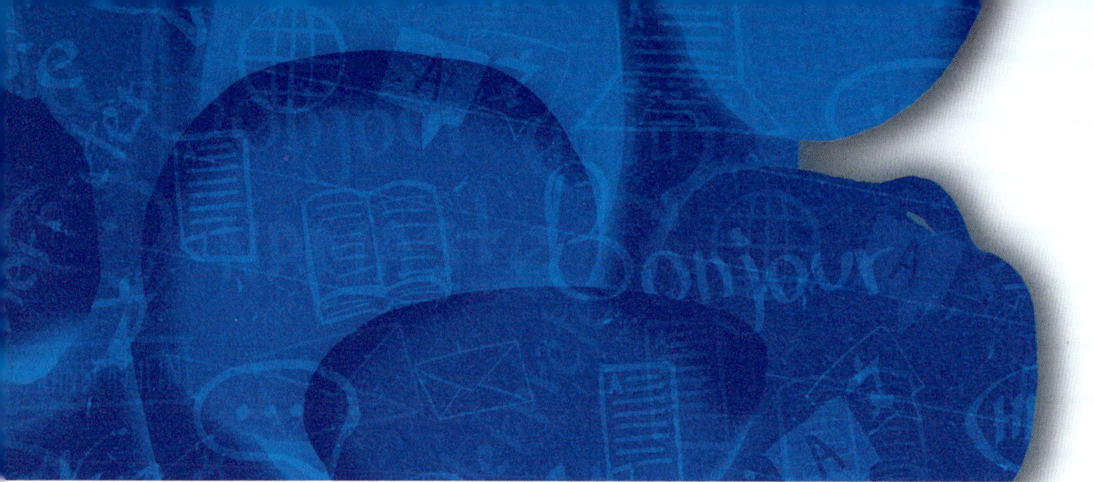

Anika is **vegetarian**. For *raat ka khaana*, she eats *roti*, *paneer*, and *daal*.

Words to Know

- रात का खाना = **dinner**
  raat ka khaana (raht kah KAH-nah)
- रोटी = **bread**
  roti (ROH-tee)
- पनीर = **cheese**
  paneer (pah-NEER)
- दाल = **lentils**
  daal (dahl)

raat ka khaana

Shubh Raatri!

Time for bed!

Kavi reads a *kahani*.

Shubh raatri!

Words to Know

- कहानी = **story**
  kahani (kah-HAH-nee)
- कंबल = **blanket**
  kambal (KAHM-bahl)
- तकिया = **pillow**
  takiya (tah-KEE-yah)
- पजामा = **pajamas**
  pajama (pah-JAH-mah)

Glossary

cricket

a field game similar to baseball that is popular in India

vegetarian

someone who does not eat meat

script

a system for writing Hindi

yoga

a type of exercise

To Learn More

AT THE LIBRARY

Davies, Monika. *India*. Minneapolis, Minn.: Bellwether Media, 2023.

Murray, Julie. *India*. Minneapolis, Minn.: ABDO Publishing Company, 2025.

Rathburn, Betsy. *Delhi*. Minneapolis, Minn.: Bellwether Media, 2024.

ON THE WEB

FACTSURFER

Factsurfer.com gives you a safe, fun way to find more information.

1. Go to www.factsurfer.com.
2. Enter "Hindi" into the search box and click 🔍.
3. Select your book cover to see a list of related content.

Index

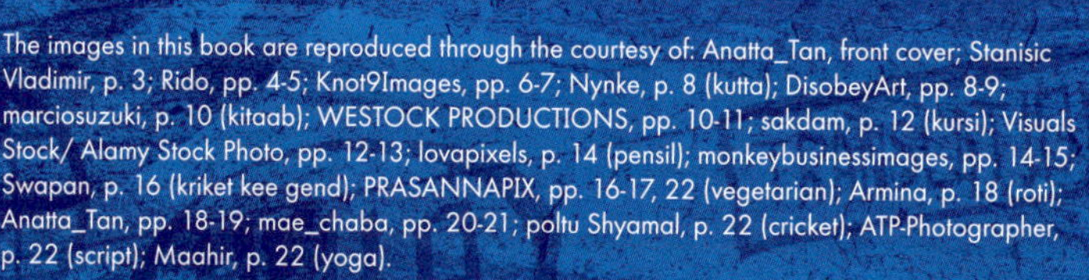

The images in this book are reproduced through the courtesy of: Anatta_Tan, front cover; Stanisic Vladimir, p. 3; Rido, pp. 4-5; Knot9Images, pp. 6-7; Nynke, p. 8 (kutta); DisobeyArt, pp. 8-9; marciosuzuki, p. 10 (kitaab); WESTOCK PRODUCTIONS, pp. 10-11; sakdam, p. 12 (kursi); Visuals Stock/ Alamy Stock Photo, pp. 12-13; lovapixels, p. 14 (pensil); monkeybusinessimages, pp. 14-15; Swapan, p. 16 (kriket kee gend); PRASANNAPIX, pp. 16-17, 22 (vegetarian); Armina, p. 18 (roti); Anatta_Tan, pp. 18-19; mae_chaba, pp. 20-21; poltu Shyamal, p. 22 (cricket); ATP-Photographer, p. 22 (script); Maahir, p. 22 (yoga).